Meet the Artist™

Édouard Manet

Melody S. Mis

PowerKiDS
press
New York

To old friends, Bonnie & Lowell Walker

Published in 2008 by The Rosen Publishing Group, Inc.
29 East 21st Street, New York, NY 10010

First Edition

Editor: Jennifer Way
Book Design: Greg Tucker
Photo Researcher: Nicole Pristash

Photo Credits: All background images © Shutterstock.com; cover © Private Collection, Peter Willi/The Bridgeman Art Library International; p. 4 © Private Collection, Archives Charmet/The Bridgeman Art Library International; p. 7 © Musée d'Orsay, Paris, France, Lauros/Giraudon/The Bridgeman Art Library International; p. 9 © Provincial Security Council, San Francisco/The Bridgeman Art Library International; p. 10 © Museu Calouste Gulbenkian, Lisbon, Portugal/The Bridgeman Art Library International; p. 12 © Museum of Fine Arts, Boston, Bequest of Sarah Choate Sears in memory of her husband/The Bridgeman Art Library International; pp. 14–15 © National Gallery, London/The Bridgeman Art Library International; p. 17 © Musee d'Orsay, Paris, France, Lauros / Giraudon / The Bridgeman Art Library International; p. 19 © Philadelphia Museum of Art/The Bridgeman Art Library International; p. 21 © Samuel Courtauld Trust, Courtauld Institute of Art Gallery/The Bridgeman Art Library International.

Library of Congress Cataloging-in-Publication Data

Mis, Melody S.
  Édouard Manet / Melody S. Mis.
     p. cm. — (Meet the artist)
  Includes index.
  ISBN-13: 978-1-4042-3841-1 (library binding)
  ISBN-10: 1-4042-3841-7 (library binding)
  1. Manet, Edouard, 1832–1883—Juvenile literature. 2. Painters—France—Biography—Juvenile literature. I. Title.
  ND553.M3M57 2007
  759.4—dc22
  [B]
                                  2007008386

Manufactured in the United States of America

CONTENTS

Édouard Manet inspired the younger impressionists to make richly colored paintings of everyday scenes.

4

Meet Édouard Manet

Édouard Manet was a French artist. He began painting in a **style** called realism. He later became known as the leader of the **impressionists**. He was called the leader of this style because he **inspired** young artists to paint everyday life in a new way.

Realist artists painted scenes exactly like they saw them, but they worked on their paintings in a **studio**. Impressionist artists painted everyday scenes, but they painted them outdoors. They copied the bold colors found in nature in their paintings. They wanted to show how sunlight changed colors.

Young Manet

Édouard Manet was born in Paris, France, on January 23, 1832. His father, Auguste, was a rich judge. His mother, Eugenie, was interested in art and music.

Manet went to school, but the only class he liked was drawing. His uncle, Charles Fournier, **encouraged** Manet's interest in art. He often took Manet to the Louvre, the largest art **museum** in Paris. After Manet finished high school, in 1848, his father wanted him to go to law school. Manet did not want to study law, so he got a job on a ship instead.

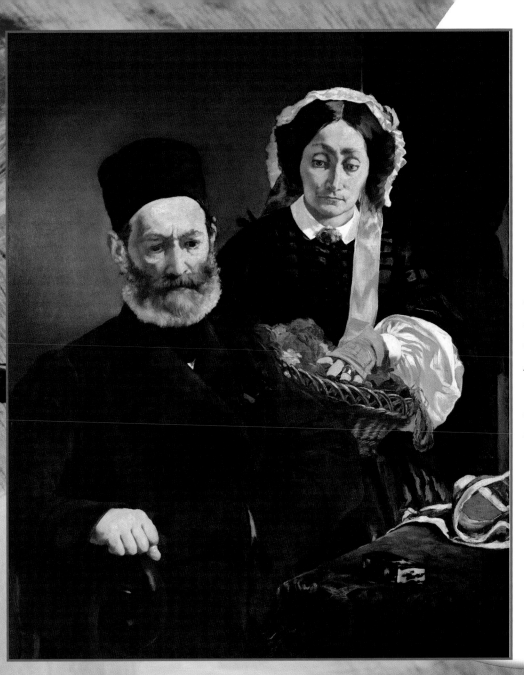

Manet painted his parents in *Portrait of Monsieur and Madame Auguste Manet* in 1860. *Monsieur* and *Madame* are the French words for "Mr." and "Mrs."

Manet's Art Education

In 1849, Manet took a test to enter the navy, but he failed it. From 1850 to 1856, he studied art with the French painter Thomas Couture. His studies included going to the Louvre and copying paintings done by the **old masters**.

During this time, Manet traveled to Italy and Germany. He visited their museums to study more artists. Manet became interested in the paintings done by the Spanish artists Diego Velázquez and Francisco José de Goya y Lucientes. These two painters inspired Manet to use simple colors and thicker dabs of paint in his own paintings.

Manet's travels in Italy inspired his paintings throughout his life. His study of other artists changed the way he used color and paint in his work. He painted *Grand Canal, Venice* in 1875.

Manet painted *The Boy with the Red Cherries* in 1859. Here you can see how he laid bright reds against the boy's dark clothes.

Manet and Realism

In 1856, Manet opened a studio, where he could paint scenes from drawings that he had made. By this time, he had stopped copying scenes from the old masters' paintings. Instead, he began to paint people and scenes that he saw around Paris. Manet's new style of painting was called realism.

Manet also changed the way he painted. He began to use brighter colors and large areas of black paint. He was more interested in how colors looked in a painting than he was in the scenes he painted.

This page: Street Singer, from 1862, is one of many Manet paintings that show everyday Parisian life.

Pages 14–15: Music in the Tuileries Gardens shows a group of people gathered to listen to music in the park. As well as his friends and family, Manet painted himself into this piece!

Music in the Tuileries Gardens

Manet spent many afternoons in the Tuileries Gardens. He made drawings of the people and the scenes that he saw there. He used the drawings as ideas for his paintings. In 1862, Manet used one of these ideas to paint *Music in the Tuileries Gardens*. It was Manet's first important painting of Parisian life. He used friends and family as models for the people in the painting.

In 1863, Manet married Suzanne Leenhoff, who had an 11-year-old son, named Leon. Manet used Leon as a model in many of his paintings.

The Paris Salon

Manet believed he would not be successful until the Paris Salon showed his work. The salon was Paris's most important art show. Many people visited the show to see and buy new paintings. The salon did not show the impressionists' paintings or most of Manet's paintings. It did not like the style of these new painters. The salon did show some of Manet's paintings, however, but not many.

In 1863, a show was held for the artists whose paintings were **rejected** by the salon. This meant that artists like Manet and the impressionists could show their work. Manet felt that this was not as good as being part of the official show at the Paris Salon.

Manet showed *The Balcony* at the 1869 Paris Salon. Most of the people who saw the painting at the salon hated it. However, Manet thought it was better to have his paintings hated at the salon rather than liked at impressionist shows.

Manet Paints Current Events

Manet was interested in what was going on all around the world. In 1864, he painted *The Battle of the "Kearsarge" and the "Alabama."* The *Kearsarge* and the *Alabama* were American ships that fought each other during America's **Civil War**. The battle took place off the coast of France, which caused the French people to take an interest in the war.

In 1870, France began a war with Germany, which lasted for six months. As soon as war broke out, Manet sent his family out of Paris before fighting reached the city. Manet served with the French army during this war.

Thousands of people watched the battle between the *Kearsarge* and the *Alabama* from the shore. Although Manet was not there, *The Battle of the "Kearsarge" and the "Alabama"* became a famous picture of the battle. He based his painting on drawings from a newspaper.

19

Manet and the Impressionists

By the 1870s, Manet had become good friends with many impressionist artists. The impressionists liked Manet's work and thought of him as their leader. They encouraged Manet to use lighter colors and to paint outdoors instead of in a studio. In 1874, Manet took his paints outside and painted the **landscapes** and street scenes in front of him.

In 1882, Manet produced his last important painting. It is called *Bar at the Folies-Bergère*. It was one of the few paintings by Manet that was shown by the Paris Salon.

Bar at the Folies-Bergère is Manet's last major work. This painting is filled with objects that were common in Parisian life at that time. An example is the different kinds of drinks shown in the painting.

Honored and Respected

Near the end of his life, Manet received an **award** from the Paris Salon for one of his paintings. He was also named to the Legion of Honor, which is France's highest award. Manet had finally become respected for his art.

In 1883, Manet's foot was **amputated** after it had become **infected**. Manet never got well after this. He died, on April 30, 1883, at the age of 51.

Manet produced 420 paintings, many of which hang in museums today. He is important because he helped change what artists paint and how they paint it.

GLOSSARY

amputated (AM-pyuh-tayt-ed) Cut off.

award (uh-WORD) A special honor given to someone.

Civil War (SIH-vul WOR) The war fought between the Northern and the Southern states of America from 1861 to 1865.

encouraged (in-KUR-ijd) Gave someone reason to do something.

impressionists (im-PREH-shuh-nists) People who make art in a style in which the subject is not as important as how the artist uses color and tone.

infected (in-FEKT-ed) Diseased.

inspired (in-SPYRD) Moved someone to do something.

landscapes (LAND-skayps) Views of places.

museum (myoo-ZEE-um) A place where art or historical pieces are safely kept for people to see and to study.

old masters (OHLD MAS-terz) Famous artists who lived a long time ago. They painted scenes from history or the Bible.

rejected (rih-JEKT-ed) Refused to take or to do something.

studio (STOO-dee-oh) A room or building where an artist works.

style (STYL) The way in which something is done.

INDEX

WEB SITES

Due to the changing nature of Internet links, PowerKids Press has developed an online list of Web sites related to the subject of this book. This site is updated regularly. Please use this link to access the list: www.powerkidslinks.com/mta/manet/